DRAWING LEGENDARY MONSTERS
DRAWING GRIFFINS
AND OTHER WINGED WONDERS

Steve Beaumont

FRANKLIN WATTS
LONDON • SYDNEY

Published in 2011 by Franklin Watts

Copyright © 2011 Arcturus Publishing Limited

Franklin Watts
338 Euston Road
London NW1 3BH

Franklin Watts Australia
Level 17/207 Kent Street
Sydney, NSW 2000

Artwork and text: Steve Beaumont and Dynamo Limited
Editors: Kate Overy and Joe Harris
Designer: Steve Flight

A CIP catalogue record for this book is available from the British Library

Dewey Decimal Classification Number: 743.8'7

ISBN: 978 1 4451 0452 2
SL001627EN

Printed in China

Franklin Watts is a division of Hachette Children's Books,
an Hachette Livre UK company.
www.hachettelivre.co.uk

CONTENTS

Getting Started 4

Inking and Colouring 5

Masterclass 6

Pegasus 8

Harpy 14

Griffin 20

Creating a Scene 26

Glossary 32

Index 32

Websites 32

GETTING STARTED

Before you can start creating fantastic artwork, you need some basic equipment. Take a look at this guide to help you get started.

PAPER

Layout Paper

It's a good idea to buy inexpensive plain A4 or A3 paper from a stationery shop for all of your practice work. Most professional illustrators use cheaper paper for basic layouts and practice sketches, before producing their final artworks on more costly material.

Cartridge Paper

This is heavy-duty, high-quality drawing paper, ideal for your final drawings. You don't have to buy the most expensive brand – most art or craft shops will stock their own brand or a student range. Unless you're thinking of turning professional, this will do just fine.

Watercolour Paper

This paper is made from 100 per cent cotton, so it is much higher quality than wood-based paper. Most art shops stock a large range of weights and sizes. Either 250 grams per square metre (gsm) or 300 gsm will be fine.

PENCILS

Buy a variety of graphite (lead) pencils ranging from soft (6B) to hard (2H). Hard pencils last longer and leave less lead on the paper. Soft pencils leave more lead and wear down quickly. HB pencils are a good medium option to start with. Spend time drawing with each pencil and get used to its qualities.

Another product to try is the mechanical pencil, where you click the lead down the barrel using the button at the top. Try 0.5 mm lead thickness to start with. These pencils are good for fine detail work.

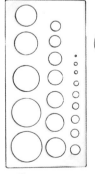

CIRCLE TEMPLATE

This is useful for drawing small circles.

FRENCH CURVES

These are available in several shapes and sizes, and are useful for drawing curves.

INKING AND COLOURING

Once you have finished your pencil drawing, you need to add ink and colour. Here are some tools you can use to achieve different results.

PENS

There are plenty of high-quality pens on the market these days that will do a decent job of inking. It's important to experiment with a range of different ones to decide which you find the most comfortable to work with.

You may find you end up using a combination of pens to produce your finished artworks. Remember to use a pen with watertight ink if you want to colour your illustrations with a watercolour or ink wash. It's usually a good idea to use watertight ink anyway as there's nothing worse than having your nicely inked drawing ruined by an accidental drop of water!

PANTONE MARKERS

These are versatile, double-ended pens that give solid, bright colours. You can use them as normal marker pens or with a brush and a little water like a watercolour pen.

BRUSHES

Some artists like to use a fine brush for inking linework. This takes a bit more practice and patience to master, but the results can be very satisfying. If you want to try your hand at brushwork, you should invest in some high-quality sable brushes.

WATERCOLOURS AND GOUACHE

Most art stores stock a wide range of these products from professional to student quality.

MASTERCLASS: DRAWING WINGS

To draw a pair of wings that look credible, it's helpful to study briefly the design of a real bird's wing.

It is not essential to learn the names of the different types of feathers and their purpose (although the more knowledge you have the better), but it is necessary to have a basic understanding of their structure. The diagram below shows the underside of a wing in detail.

UNDERSIDE OF WING

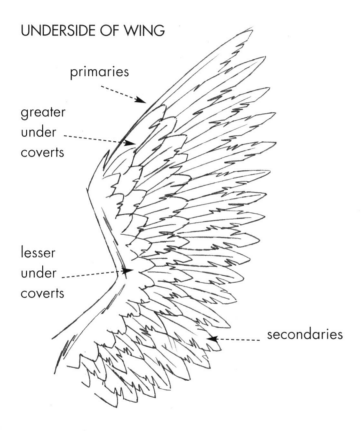

primaries

greater under coverts

lesser under coverts

secondaries

DRAWING THE WING

Picture 1 As a starting point for drawing a wing, begin with a stick drawing that loosely resembles an arm.

Picture 2 Now gauge where the three layers of feathers will sit.

Picture 3 Then add the primary and secondary feathers.

Picture 4 Next draw the coverts. Finally add some detail and now you have a wing that's ready to ink.

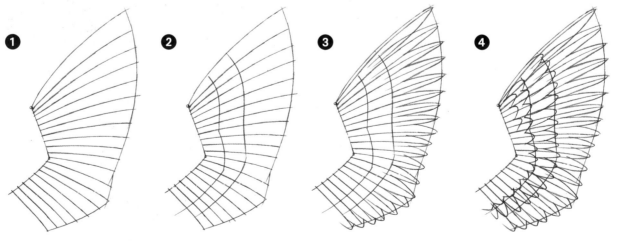

❶ ❷ ❸ ❹

MASTERCLASS: HARPY'S FACE

Here we'll give more detail on constructing the head of the harpy from pages 14–19.

Picture 1 Construct the head of the harpy.

Picture 2 Draw the features of the face. Note the large, thin hook nose that is almost beak-like and the pointy cheek bones.

Picture 3 Add the shape of the hair, which is almost like that of a wobbly teardrop. It is best to start with a simple, uncomplicated shape to establish the flow of the hair.

Picture 4 Now add detail to the hair, teeth and mouth.

Picture 5 Finally, shade in the hair and face and the harpy's head is complete.

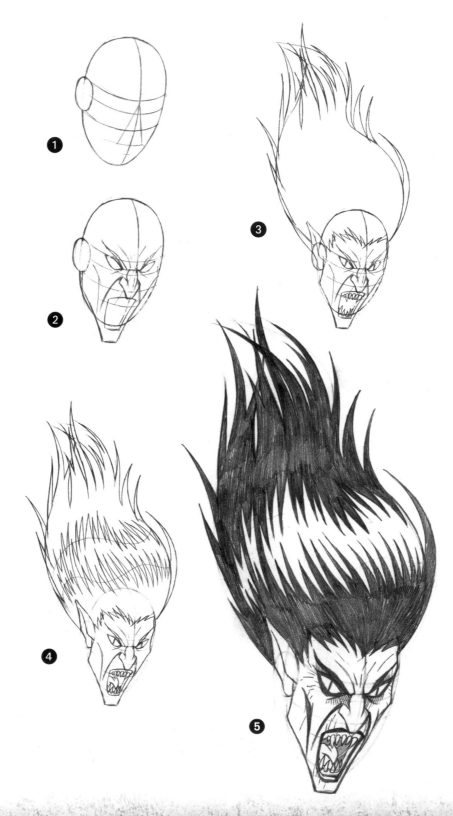

PEGASUS

Winged creatures have been the stuff of legend the world over for centuries. Pegasus is the winged horse that sprang from the blood of Medusa, and he has been the steed of many brave warriors and adventurers. His first and most famous rider was Perseus, the heroic son of the Greek god Zeus.

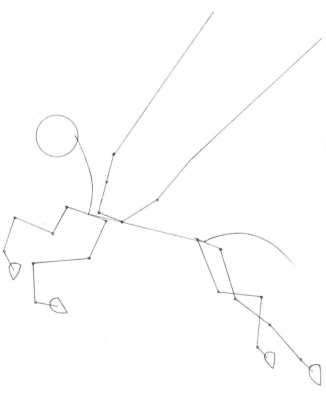

1
Start with the stick figure. Draw the horse's body and legs in the correct positions. Include long straight lines for the wings.

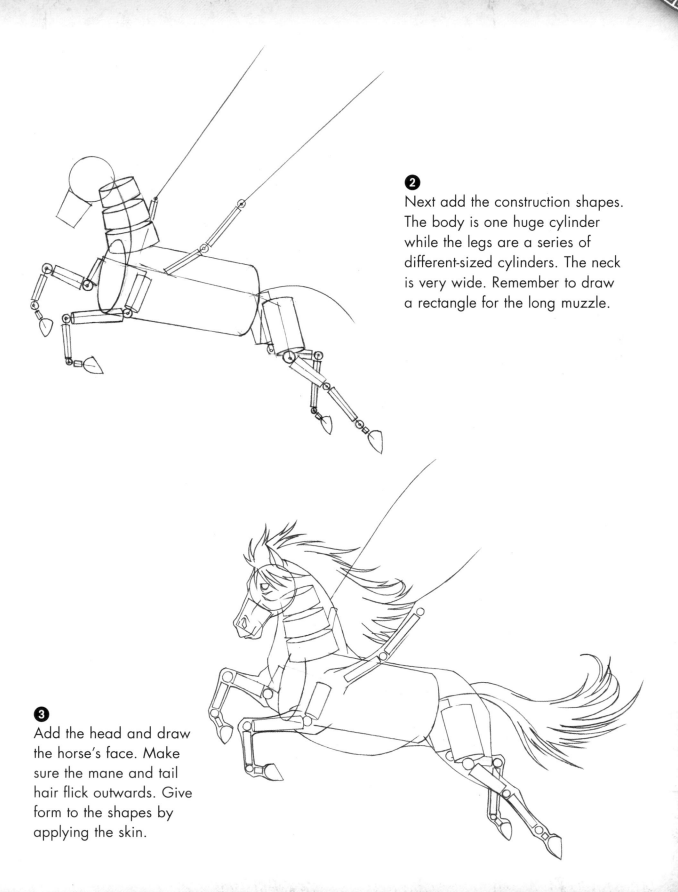

2
Next add the construction shapes. The body is one huge cylinder while the legs are a series of different-sized cylinders. The neck is very wide. Remember to draw a rectangle for the long muzzle.

3
Add the head and draw the horse's face. Make sure the mane and tail hair flick outwards. Give form to the shapes by applying the skin.

4

Now remove the construction
lines and add the wings.

*You'll find detailed
instructions on how
to draw wings on
page 6.*

5

Give the wings texture with some shading and add detail to the face and body. Notice how we have used cross-hatching for shading in various places.

TOP TIP
By inking the contours of the neck with solid thick lines, you can really make Pegasus's muscles stand out and emphasise his strength.

❻
Ink over the final pencil drawing. Use solid black where the mane and tail join the body to add depth.

7

Colour this drawing using the palest grey base across the whole image.

When colouring the wings, mane and tail, use darker blue and lilac. Add grey to give definition.

Apply a slightly darker grey to the belly, legs and underside of the neck to create form. Build up the layers with light blue and mauve.

The hooves are grey with hints of mauve.

HARPY

The most terrifying of all flying creatures is the harpy. Half-woman, half-bird, she is like something from a nightmare – screeching, filthy and constantly on the lookout for weak and vulnerable prey to slice apart with her long talons.

1
Draw the stick figure. Plot lines for the huge wings and include a curved tail. The harpy is diving and about to grab her prey.

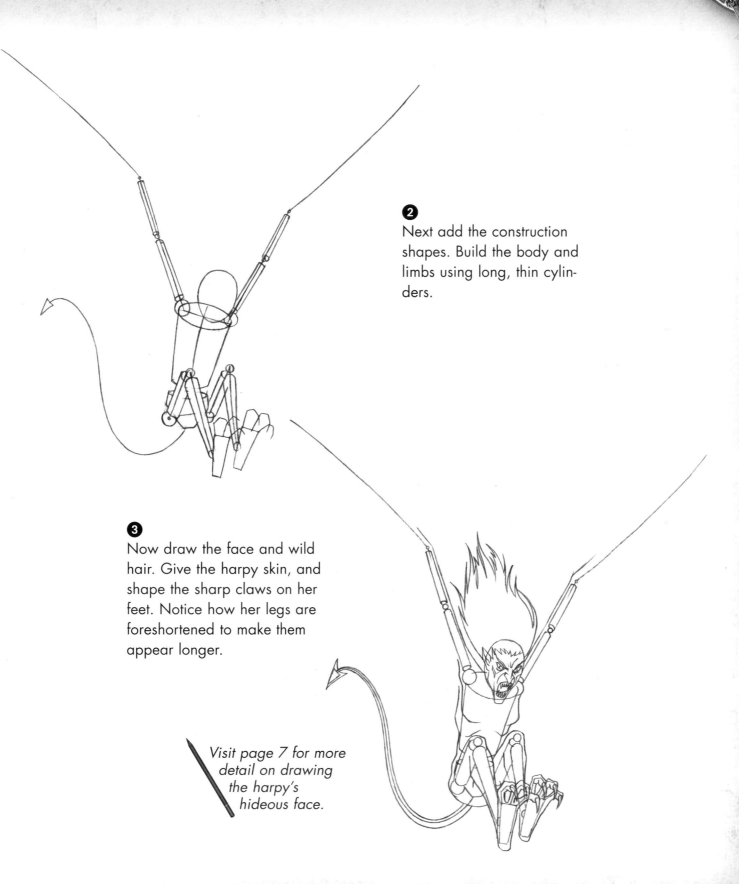

2
Next add the construction shapes. Build the body and limbs using long, thin cylinders.

3
Now draw the face and wild hair. Give the harpy skin, and shape the sharp claws on her feet. Notice how her legs are foreshortened to make them appear longer.

Visit page 7 for more detail on drawing the harpy's hideous face.

4

Add the wings and feathers, then erase the construction shapes. Remember to include feathers on the harpy's upper body.

TOP TIP
When creating your harpy, imagine her as an evil, wizened old witch to help you bring out this mood in the final artwork.

5
Apply shading to the feathers to create depth and form. Add wrinkles to the legs and feet to give the skin texture. When shading in the hair, leave an area of white to act as a highlight.

6

Ink over the pencil drawing, remembering to keep the highlights on the hair and claws. Notice how the solid block of shading behind the harpy's legs makes her feet leap out of the picture.

Harpy

❼
Colour the evil witch-like harpy to make her even more hideous. Start with a pale yellow-green base.

Build up the feathered body and wings with emerald green, darker green and blue-green.

For the legs, feet and face, apply a flesh tone. Follow this with layers of pale green, yellow and grey to create a sickly appearance.

GRIFFIN

The most noble of winged creatures is the griffin. This powerful and courageous monster is part-eagle and part-lion. According to legend, the griffin's bones were so strong that humans once used its ribs to make bows.

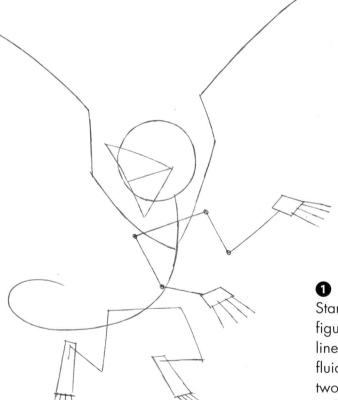

1
Start with the stick figure. Try to draw the line for the spine in one fluid movement. Include two triangles for the griffin's beak.

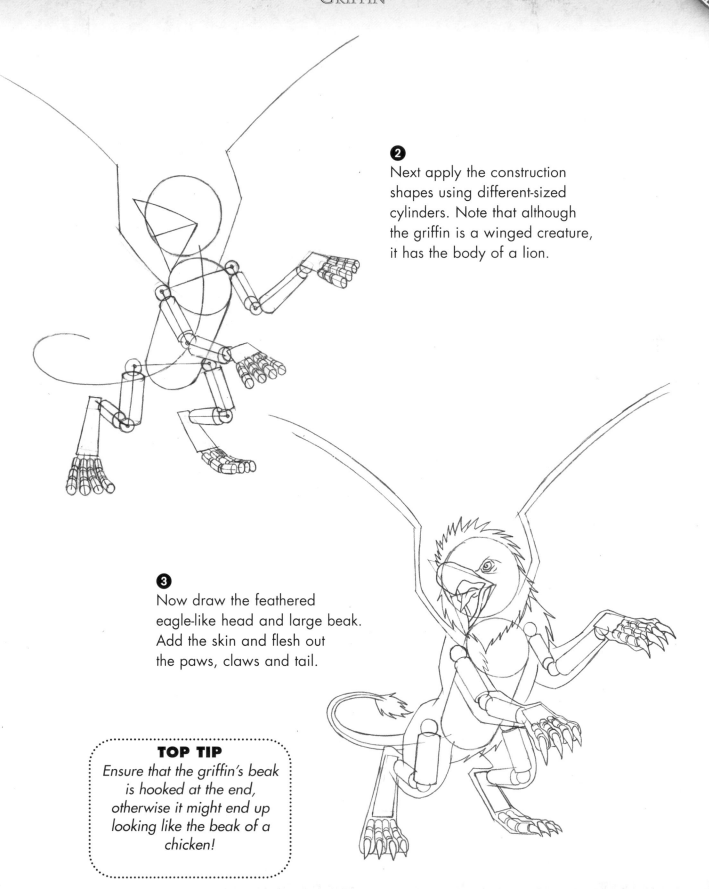

2

Next apply the construction shapes using different-sized cylinders. Note that although the griffin is a winged creature, it has the body of a lion.

3

Now draw the feathered eagle-like head and large beak. Add the skin and flesh out the paws, claws and tail.

TOP TIP
Ensure that the griffin's beak is hooked at the end, otherwise it might end up looking like the beak of a chicken!

Go to page 6 for more instructions on how to draw wings.

❹
Erase the construction shapes and add the wings and feathers. Notice how the feathers get longer in each layer.

5 Now add the detail to finalise your pencil drawing. Include shading on the wings to create definition. Use cross-hatching for this.

6

Apply ink over the pencil drawing.
Take care to keep the delicate
quality of the cross-hatching.

GRIFFIN

7

Your griffin will look magnificent when you go over it in colour.

Use a light grey base for the head and wings, followed by layers of darker grey with splashes of ice blue. Also add a hint of beige.

Give the beak a yellow base and add orange for the shading.

The lion's body has a sandy beige base. On top of that use a darker sandy tone and light brown.

25

CREATING A SCENE: GUARDIAN GRIFFIN

The griffin makes the perfect guard, since it is as sharp-eyed as an eagle, as fearless as a lion, and many times more dangerous than either! In this scene, the griffin watches over a partially damaged fortress, protecting its inhabitants from dark forces.

1 Drawing lines of perspective and a vanishing point will help you to keep everything to scale, and give your image a sense of depth. In this scene, the perspective lines meet in a vanishing point on the right-hand side of the image.

2 Sketch out the mountain range in the background. Creating layers of mountains – some nearer, some further away – will work much better than a single cliff face. Now you can also roughly mark out where you want to place your castle ruins.

3 Begin fleshing out your fort and the mountains. Adding small details into any blank areas of the mountains will help break them up and make them look more natural. But don't go overboard – too much background detail may detract from your main character.

4 When shading, it's vital to bear in mind the location of your light source, along with how the shadows will fall. Pay attention to how certain mountains will affect the light that is shed on your ruins, or other mountains in the range.

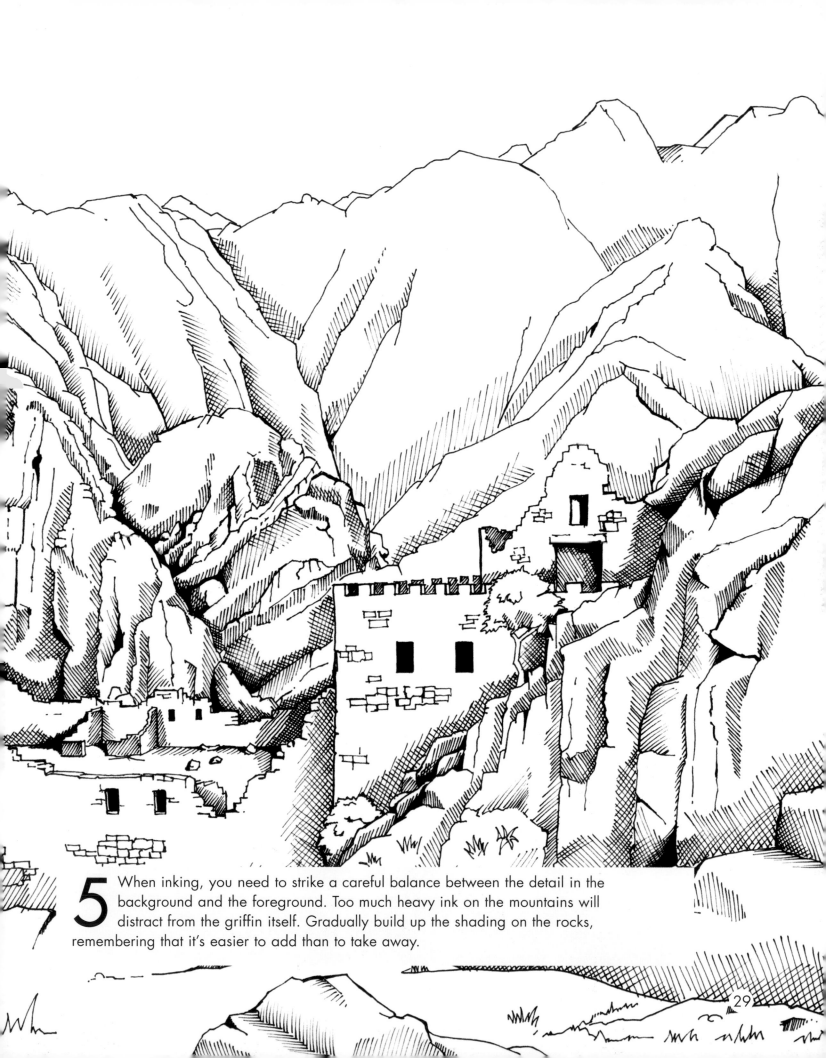

5 When inking, you need to strike a careful balance between the detail in the background and the foreground. Too much heavy ink on the mountains will distract from the griffin itself. Gradually build up the shading on the rocks, remembering that it's easier to add than to take away.

6 You have two main options when colouring this scene. Either you can use yellow and brown tones to create a bleak, barren mountaintop in a desert-like setting. Or you can go with the option we've chosen here, of using a greener colour palette to suggest a more lush and temperate climate.

GLOSSARY

cross-hatching
A shading technique where criss-crossing diagonal lines are overlapped to make an area of shadow.

cuboid
An object that has six faces like a cube.

cylinder
A shape with circular ends and straight sides.

foreshortening
In art, making something shorter to show that it is angled towards the viewer.

perspective
Changing the size and shape of objects in an artwork to create a sense of nearness or distance.

temperate
With a mild climate.

vanishing point
The point at which the lines showing perspective in a drawing meet each other.

wizened
Creased up with age.

INDEX

B
Beak 20, 21, 25
Brushes 5

C
Castle 26–31
Claws 15, 18, 21
Colouring 5
Cross-hatching 11, 23, 24

E
Equipment 4–5

F
Feathers 6, 16, 17, 19, 21, 22

G
Gouache 5
Griffin 20–25, 26–31

H
Harpy 7, 14–19
Hooves 13
Horse 8–13

I
Inking 5

L
Lion 20, 21, 25, 26

M
Mane 9, 12, 13
Mountains 26–31

P
Paper 4
Pegasus 8–13
Pencils 4
Pens 5
Perspective 26

R
Ruins 26

T
Tail 9, 12, 13, 14, 21
Teeth 7

V
Vanishing point 26

W
Watercolours 5
Wings 6, 8, 10, 11, 13, 14, 15, 16, 19, 20, 21, 22, 23, 25

WEBSITES

http://www.elfwood.com/farp/art.html
A collection of articles about drawing characters and scenes from myth and fantasy.

http://drawsketch.about.com/od/drawfantasyandscifi/tp/imagination.htm
Advice on drawing from your imagination.